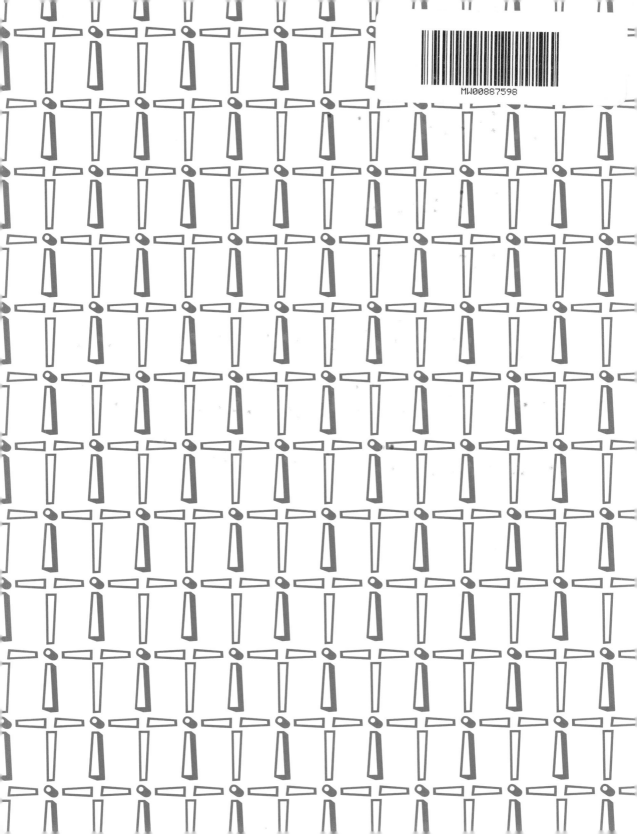

Advent 2015

To Emrie
Love Tia

May God bless you and
keep you, this Advent and
always! I love you. XO

The Holy Moly Christmas Story

BY REBECCA GLASER
ILLUSTRATED BY BILL FERENC AND EMMA TRITHART

SPARK HOUSE FAMILY

MINNEAPOLIS

Contents

Book design by Toolbox Studios, Dave Wheeler, Alisha Lofgren, Janelle Markgren, and Ivy Palmer Skrade
Colorization: Dave Wheeler

Library of Congress Cataloging-in-Publication Data

Glaser, Rebecca Stromstad, author.
  The Holy Moly Christmas story / by Rebecca Glaser ; illustrated by Bill Ferenc and Emma Trithart.
      pages cm. — (Holy Moly Bible storybooks)
  Summary: "An illustrated retelling of the story of Christmas."— Provided by publisher.
  Audience: Ages 5-8
  Audience: K to grade 3
  ISBN 978-1-5064-0257-4 (alk. paper)
1. Jesus Christ—Nativity—Juvenile literature. 2. Bible. Gospels—Juvenile literature. 3. Bible stories, English—Gospels—Juvenile literature. 4. Christmas—Juvenile literature. I. Ferenc, Bill, illustrator. II. Trithart, Emma, illustrator. III. Title.
  BT315.3.G53 2015
  232.92—dc23
                                  2015020848
Printed on acid-free paper

Printed in U.S.A.

24 23 22 21 20 19 18 17 16 15   1 2 3 4 5 6 7 8 9 10

V63474; 9781506402574; OCT2015

The Angel Speaks to Mary

Mary lived in the town of Nazareth.
She was engaged to a man named Joseph.

Whoosh Whoosh.
One day, an angel appeared to Mary.

"Greetings!"
the angel Gabriel said.

Mary's heart pounded.
She gasped with fear.
Who was this? And why
was he talking to HER?

4

"Do not be afraid, Mary, for you have found favor with God," Gabriel said. "You will have a son. His name will be Jesus."

Mary was surprised! But she trusted God.

God sent an angel to Joseph in a dream. "Do not be afraid, Joseph," the angel told him. "Take Mary as your wife. She will have a son, and you will name him Jesus."

Mary and Joseph were nervous, but they knew God was with them. They prepared for the birth of God's Son.

Mary and Elizabeth

While Mary was pregnant, she set out to visit her relative Elizabeth. Even though Elizabeth was very old, God had promised she would have a baby too!

Mary walked and walked along the road, through towns and past houses, until she arrived at Elizabeth's house in a town in the hill country of Judea.

Color the
path Mary
took.

When Elizabeth saw Mary, the baby inside her jumped for joy. "Mary, you are blessed!" Elizabeth exclaimed. "You're going to have God's Son!"

Mary stayed with Elizabeth for about three months. Elizabeth gave birth to a son and named him John. When John grew up, many people called him John the Baptist.

Jesus Is Born

On the night Jesus was born, there were shepherds nearby. They watched over their flocks of sheep in the fields outside Bethlehem.

Mary and Joseph were in Bethlehem for the census, just like many, many other people. All the inns were full, so Mary and Joseph stayed in a stable with animals nearby.

Baby Jesus was born that night. Mary wrapped him in cloth and laid him in a manger.

WHOOSH! An angel appeared before the shepherds in the field. They were frightened and tried to hide!

Just then the sky was FILLED with angels singing, "Glory to God and peace on Earth!"

The shepherds hurried off to find the new baby— the Messiah!

At the humble stable, the
shepherds found the baby Jesus,
Mary, and Joseph. They peeked
at the baby's tiny hands. They
smiled at the baby's little toes.
They were amazed. Jesus, God's
Son, had been born!

The Wise Men Follow the Star

A long way from Bethlehem, some wise men were watching the stars. Suddenly, they saw something surprising. A new star was rising! It was a sign that a special king had been born for God's people.

The wise men traveled to Jerusalem in search of the new king. They wanted to visit the child and honor him.

King Herod was jealous when he heard. A new king? Herod wanted to be the ONLY king! He searched high and low to find out where this new king was.

Herod called the wise men. "Go to Bethlehem and find this new king," he told them.

"Then come back and
tell me where he is.
I want to honor him too."

The wise men followed the star to Bethlehem. It shone high in the sky over a little house where Jesus, Mary, and Joseph were staying.

Color in the map.

When the wise men saw Jesus, they welcomed and honored him with gifts of gold, frankincense, and myrrh. In a dream, they were warned not to tell Herod where the child was, so they went home by a different route.

More Activities

LOOK AND FIND

Find the

in The Angel Speaks to Mary on pages 3–8.

Mary and Joseph promised to get married to each other.

Find

in the Mary and Elizabeth story on pages 9–14.

Elizabeth was Mary's older cousin. She was surprised by having a baby too!

Find the

in the Jesus Is Born story on pages 15–22.

The shepherds were surprised when a crowd of angels burst into the sky. Shepherds were usually the last ones to hear important news.

Find the

in The Wise Men Follow the Star on pages 23–30.

The Wise Men followed this star all the way from Persia to find the baby king Jesus.

ACTION PRAYER

Dear God,

We crouch like a shepherd. *(bend knees to a crouch)*

We are frightened by the light. *(shield eyes with hands)*

We stand up for Mary *(stand up)*, who did what was right. *(thumbs up)*

We sit down by the manger, smile right along. *(sit cross-legged and smile)*

We jump for Jesus! *(jump up high)* We twirl for joy! *(spin around)*

Christmas brings us a special boy. *(bend arms into cradling motion)*

Amen!

MATCHING GAME

Match the person from the Bible with the fact about them.

1. I was a young woman chosen by God to give birth to Jesus.

2. I am one of only two angels mentioned by name in the Bible.

3. My name in Greek could mean carpenter, metal worker, or artist.

4. We were philosophers who studied the stars. We followed one to find Jesus.

5. My baby jumped inside me when I heard Mary's good news.

6. I am Emmanuel, which means "God with us."

7. We were surprised when the angels came to us.

8. We are powerful, unearthly messengers.

1. Mary; 2. Gabriel; 3. Joseph; 4. Wise Men; 5. Elizabeth; 6. Baby Jesus; 7. Shepherds; 8. Angels